The MAILBOX® The Education Center®

Organize FEBRUARY Now!™

Everything You Need for a Successful February

Monthly Organizing Tools
Manage your time, classroom, and students with monthly organizational tools.

Thematic Idea Collections
Practice essential skills this month with engaging activities and reproducibles.

February in the Classroom
Carry your monthly themes into every corner of the classroom.

Ready-to-Go Learning Centers and Skills Practice
Bring February to life right now!

D1105414

Managing Editor: Allison E. Ward

Editorial Team: Becky S. Andrews, Kimberley Bruck, Karen P. Shelton, Diane Badden, Thad H. McLaurin, Sharon Murphy, Cindy K. Daoust, Gerri Primak, Karen A. Brudnak, Hope Rodgers, Dorothy C. McKinney, Janet Boyce, Jill Davis, Roxanne LaBell Dearman, Danna De Mars, Deborah Garmon, Ada Goren, Lucia Kemp Henry, Cynthia Holcomb, Patricia Kessler, Julie Koczur, Angie Kutzer, Linda Lawson, Jan McCosker, Ann Miller, Heather Miller, Keely Peasner, Deborah Ryan, Andrea Singleton, Valerie Wood Smith, Susan Walker

Production Team: Lisa K. Pitts, Pam Crane, Rebecca Saunders, David G. Bullard, Jennifer Tipton Cappoen, Chris Curry, Sarah Foreman, Theresa Lewis Goode, Clint Moore, Greg D. Rieves, Barry Slate, Donna K. Teal, Zane Williard, Tazmen Carlisle, Cat Collins, Marsha Heim, Amy Kirtley-Hill, Lynette Dickerson, Mark Rainey, Angela Kamstra, Debbie Shoffner

www.themailbox.com

Manufactured in the United States
10 9 8 7 6 5 4 3 2

Table of Contents

Monthly Organizing Tools

A collection of reproducible forms, notes, and other timesavers and organizational tools just for February.

Thematic Idea Collections

Fun, child-centered ideas for your favorite February themes.

February in the Classroom

In a hurry to find a specific type of February activity? It's right here!

Ready-to-Go Learning Centers and Skills Practice

Two center activities you can tear out and use today! Plus a collection of February-themed reproducibles for fine-motor skills practice!

Skills Grid

	Groundhog Day	Valentine's Day	Presidents' Day	Dental Health	Centers	Circle Time & Games	Learning Center: Where's the Candy?	Learning Center: Sounds Like Tooth	Ready-to-Go Skills Practice
Literacy									
identifying color words		23							
skills review		26							
beginning sound /h/		33							
beginning sound /v/		34							
print awareness			36						
beginning sound /t/				49				82	
beginning sound /sh/					60				
matching lowercase letters					61				
positional words *in* and *out*							74		
Language Development									
oral language	18			43					
descriptive language				44					
Math									
visual discrimination	21	32							
matching numbers		22							
one-to-one correspondence		25							
skills review		26							
shapes		31							
sorting			37						
color recognition			38						
number sets				42					
sorting by color					60				
matching sets					62				
number awareness						66			
counting						67			
Science									
observe changes in materials		24							
data collection				45					
Physical Health & Development									
fine-motor skills		22	36	45	61, 62				
gross-motor skills		24							
nutrition				42					
oral hygiene				43					
tracing									
cut and glue									90, 91, 92 93, 94, 95, 96
Creative Arts									
use a variety of materials		23							
participate in song		25							
dramatic play		26							
painting			37						
drawing			38						
Social & Emotional Development									
self-esteem						66			
understanding feelings						67			
Approaches to Learning									
predictions	18								
memory				44					

Awards: Use these awards to reinforce positive behaviors.

Medallion
Tape to a child's clothing or
to a crepe paper necklace.

Wristband
Write a skill in the space. Tape the ends together where shown.

Tape here.

I'm brushing up on…

Headband
Glue to a construction paper strip
sized to fit around a child's head.

I Deserve a Hug!

Ask
me
why!

©The Mailbox® • *Organize February Now!*™ • TEC60970

Brag tags: Copy the tags on colorful construction paper and use as desired.

Monthly Organizing Tools 5

February

Sunday	Monday	Tuesday	Wednesday	Thursday	Friday	Saturday

Center Checklist

Name

Center

CLASS LIST

Candy

NAME													

Classroom News

From _____

Date _____

Special Thanks

Help Wanted

Look What We Are Learning

☆ Superstars ☆

Please Remember

9

Classroom News

From _____

Date _____

You're sweet!

Special Delivery

TEC60970

Clip art: Use the artwork on student papers and on correspondence such as announcements, forms, and parent notes.

Meetings:

Duties This Month:

Materials to Collect:

Birthdays & Special Dates:

Themes:

To Do:

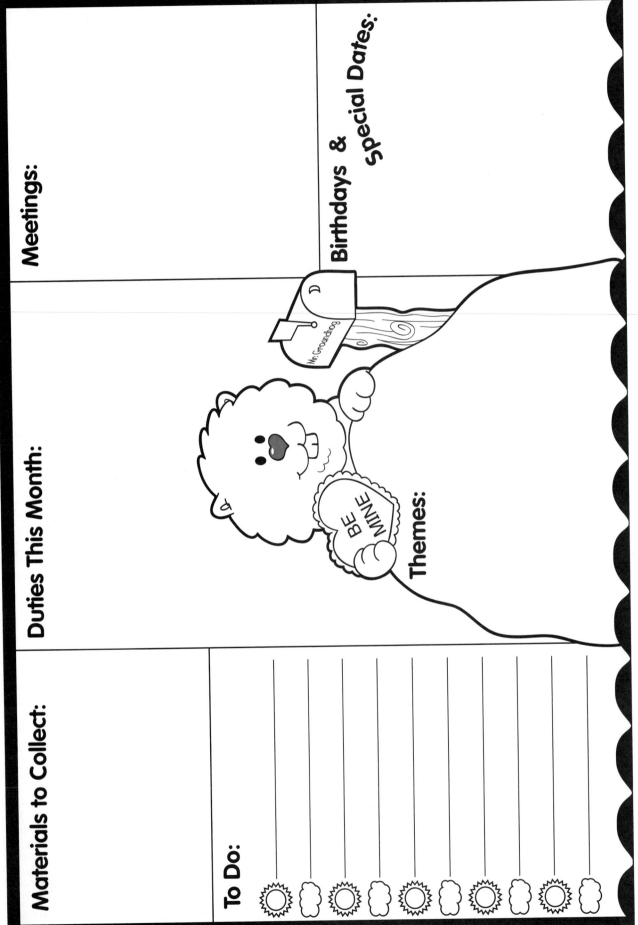

Mr. Groundhog

BE MINE

Monthly planning form: Use this handy form to stay on top of February's school-related responsibilities.

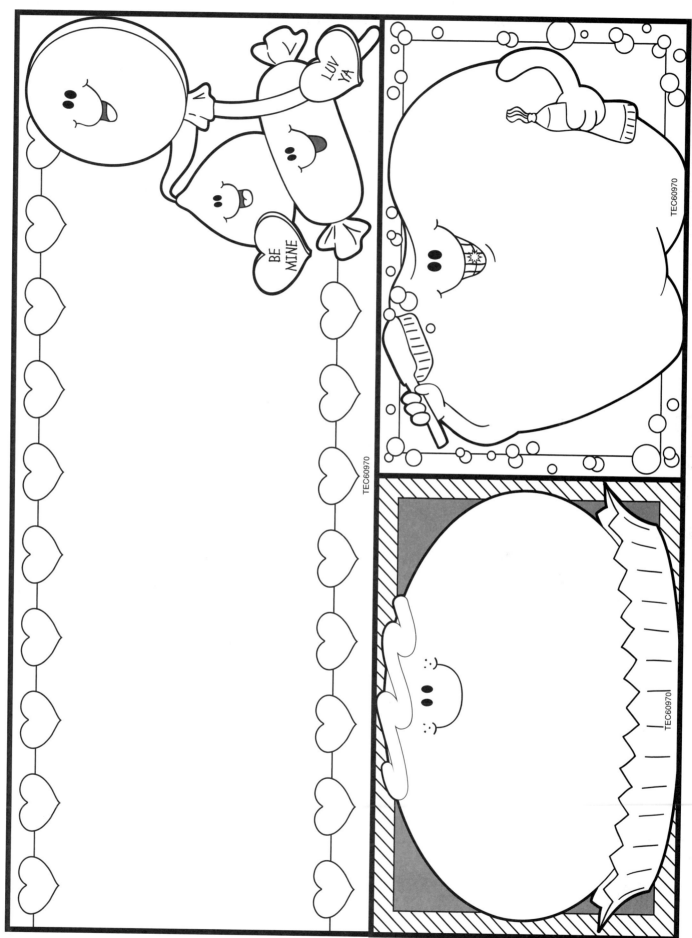

Table and cubby tags: Copy these tags on construction paper and personalize them with your youngsters' names. If desired, laminate the tags for durability.

©The Mailbox® • *Organize February Now!*™ • TEC60970

Open: Use this page for parent correspondence or use it with students. For example, ask a child to draw a valentine treat or have her dictate a valentine message to a friend or loved one.

_____
date

Dear Parent,

   Please remember

Parent reminder note: Use this note to remind parents of supply requests, field trips, and special events such as classroom parties, school programs, or guest speakers.

School Note

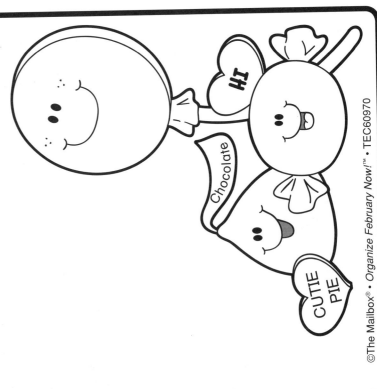

SCHOOL NOTE

©The Mailbox® • *Organize February Now!*™ • TEC60970

School notes: Use these notes for parent communications such as announcing an upcoming event, requesting supplies or volunteers, and writing messages of praise.

Family Fun

You will love working with your child to complete this heartfelt project! Please help your child draw a picture of himself or herself in the center of the heart. Then have him or her color the outer edge of the heart as desired.

We hope to see your project by _____.

Sincerely,

Learning Link: develops fine-motor skills

Note to the teacher: Date and sign a copy of the page. Then make student copies on construction paper. Write a child's name on the back of a heart before sending it home with him. When he returns his project, cut out his artwork and add it to a display titled "Guess Who Loves You!" Then invite youngsters to guess whom each heart belongs to.

Groundhog Day

Whether or not the groundhog sees its shadow, fun learning activities are popping up in this unit!

Language Development

Oral language

Shadow Spotting

According to legend, the groundhog emerges from its burrow on February 2 to look for its shadow. Introduce youngsters to the groundhog's yearly tradition with this little ditty! Cut out a copy of the groundhog puppet on page 19 for each child. Have her color the groundhog's face brown and color the face outline (shadow) black. Fold the puppet along the thin line and glue a large craft stick between the two sides. Then sing the song shown and invite youngsters to hold their puppets, showing the appropriate side for each verse.

(sung to the tune of "Where Is Thumbkin?")

Where's my shadow? Where's my shadow?
It's not here! It's not here!
Spring is on its way. Spring is on its way.
Run and play. Run and play.

Where's my shadow? Where's my shadow?
Here it is! Here it is!
Six more weeks of winter. Six more weeks of winter.
Run and hide. Run and hide.

Approaches to Learning

Predictions

Out of the Hole

Prior to Groundhog Day, have each child predict whether or not the groundhog will see its shadow. For each student, cut out a copy of the patterns on page 20. Help him write his prediction to complete the sentence. Then have him color the patterns and glue them to a 3" x 24" tagboard strip. Next, fit the headband to his head and secure the ends. On Groundhog Day, encourage little ones to don their headbands as you reveal whether or not the groundhog saw its shadow. Then invite youngsters to compare their predictions to the result.

The groundhog _____ will not _____ see its shadow.

Find a reproducible activity on page 21.

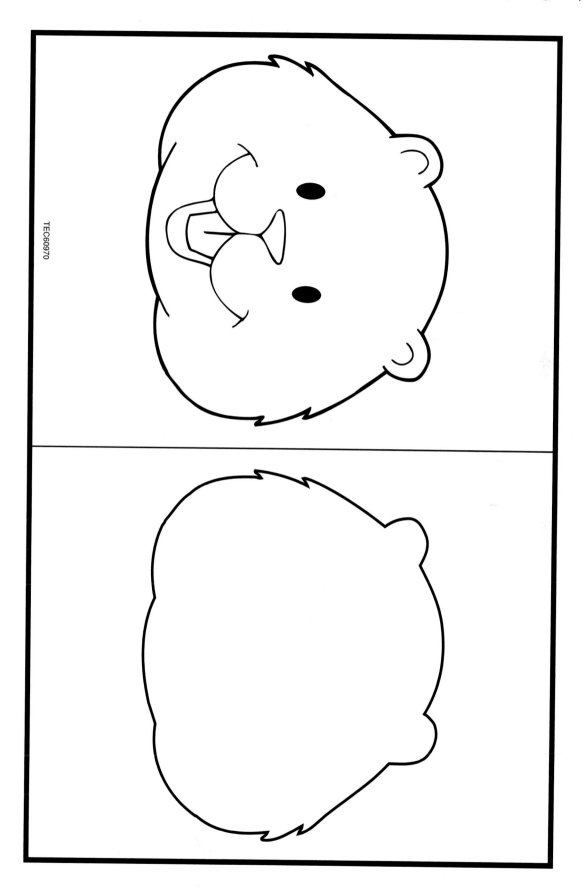

TEC60970

Headband Patterns

Use with "Out of the Hole" on page 18.

The groundhog _____ see its shadow.

TEC60970

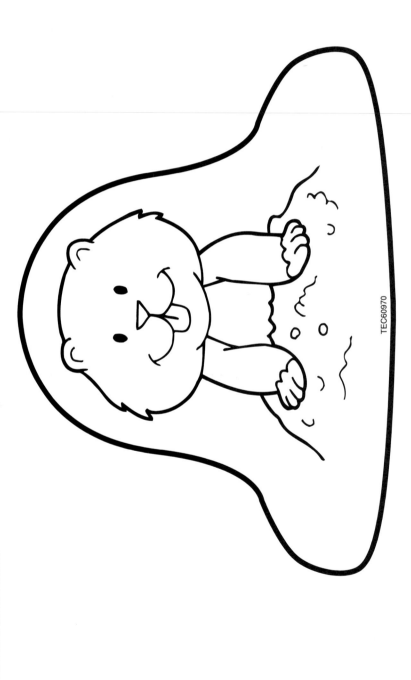

TEC60970

Groundhogs in Motion

Name _____

 Draw a line to make a match.

Valentine's Day

Fine-motor skills

Chain of Love

Little fingers get a workout with this pretty paper chain. Give each child a 1½" x 12" strip of construction paper in a valentine color, such as red, pink, purple, or white. Invite her to decorate the strip. Then help each child, in turn, staple her strip into a link to create a class chain as shown. Hang the chain over your door for a lovely Valentine's Day decoration.

Matching numbers

Math

Centered on Hearts

Remove the numbered heart cards from an old deck of playing cards. Cut each card in half with a different simple puzzle cut; then place the pieces in a center. Ask a child to assemble each puzzle, making sure the numbers on each card half match. For an added challenge, have students identify the numbers as they work.

Get to the heart of preschool learning with these sweet activities!

Creative Arts

Use a variety of materials

Lovebugs

This art project makes a sweet card for loved ones! To make one, a child chooses a 12" x 18" sheet of construction paper in a valentine color. He sponge-prints hearts in an alternating color pattern. When the paint is dry, he uses a thin black marker to add a face, legs, and antennae (as shown). If desired, have him add two heart stickers to the ends of the antennae and color green grass at the bottom of the paper. Help him glue on a copy of the hearts on page 27 to complete the project.

This little lovebug is here to say,

"Have a happy Valentine's Day!"

Literacy

Identifying color words

Colorful Hearts

Here's a rhyming booklet that will have youngsters seeing red, yellow, green, and blue! For each child, cut apart a copy of the booklet cover and booklet pages on pages 28–30 and staple them in order to make a booklet. As you read the booklet aloud, have each child color the heart on pages 1–4 to correspond with the color word. Next, have students color the hearts on the cover and the last page with all the colors in the booklet. Enlist students' help to reread the booklet; then send the booklets home so that little ones can share their color knowledge with their families.

HEARTS

by Tamika

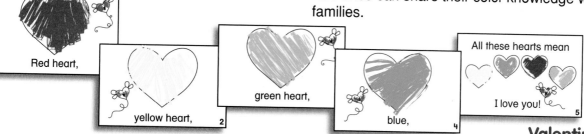

Red heart,

yellow heart, 2

green heart,

blue, 4

All these hearts mean

I love you! 5

Science

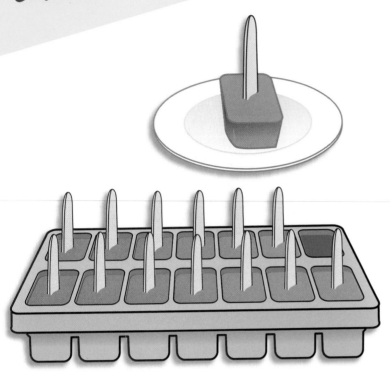

Valentine Pops

Invite youngsters to observe as you pour a large box of instant vanilla pudding mix into a large lidded container. Then add milk as directed on the package. Have each child take a turn shaking the pudding mixture until it thickens. Ask youngsters to tell you how the mixture has changed. Then add red food coloring and shake again. Now how has the mixture changed? Spoon the mixture into ice cube trays, cover them with aluminum foil, and insert a clean craft stick into each cup of the tray. Freeze the trays for at least four hours. Pop out the frozen treats and invite each child to enjoy one. Don't forget to ask students to describe how the mixture changed!

Gross-motor skills

Physical Health & Development

Hearty Moves

Get little hearts pumping with this movement activity! Give each child a paper heart to put on the floor in front of her. Teach youngsters the rhyme shown, and ask them to march around their paper hearts when cued. Then repeat the rhyme, substituting a different action for the word *march*, such as *hop, jump, tiptoe, run, dance,* or *twist.*

Up on your toes,
Then bend your knees.
[March] around your heart now
If you please!

Creative Arts

Friends and Valentines

Gather your class in a circle to sing this action song that celebrates friendship!

(sung to the tune of "This Little Light of Mine")

These little friends of mine,	*Point to others in the group.*
They're all my valentines!	*Point thumb to self.*

Repeat three times.

Hello, friends!	*Wave at friends.*
You are my	*Point to friends, then self.*
Valentines!	*Put hands over heart.*

Math • • • • • • • • • • • • • • • One-to-one correspondence

Sweet Treats

Around Valentine's Day, heart-shaped boxes of candy are everywhere, so why not use a few to strengthen math skills? Place a matching number of small, empty candy boxes and large brown pom-poms (chocolates) in a center. Invite a child to pretend to be a valentine candy maker and use one-to-one correspondence to place one chocolate in each box. For more advanced preschoolers, vary the number of chocolates and candy boxes. Ask each candy maker to complete the center and then use terms such as *more, less,* and *same as* to describe the outcome for you.

Creative Arts

Hearts and Flowers

Create a flower shop where your youngsters can make beautiful bouquets for Valentine's Day! Stock your dramatic-play area with artificial flowers, plastic vases or empty water bottles, tissue paper for wrapping bouquets, plastic flowerpots, paper and pencils for taking orders, and heart cutouts for cards. Add a toy cash register and phone if desired. Then invite little ones to pretend to be customers and workers getting ready for the holiday.

Literacy or Math

Skills review

Chocolate Scribbles

Try this yummy way to review letters, shapes, or numbers! Give each child a squirt of chocolate Reddi-wip whipped topping on a foam plate. Invite him to smooth out the whipped cream with freshly washed hands and then use a fingertip to write letters or numbers or to draw shapes. If desired, give each child a chocolate graham cracker stick to use as a writing tool. Wrap up the activity by inviting youngsters to lick their fingers before giving their hands a more thorough washing at the sink.

Find reproducible activities on pages 31–35.

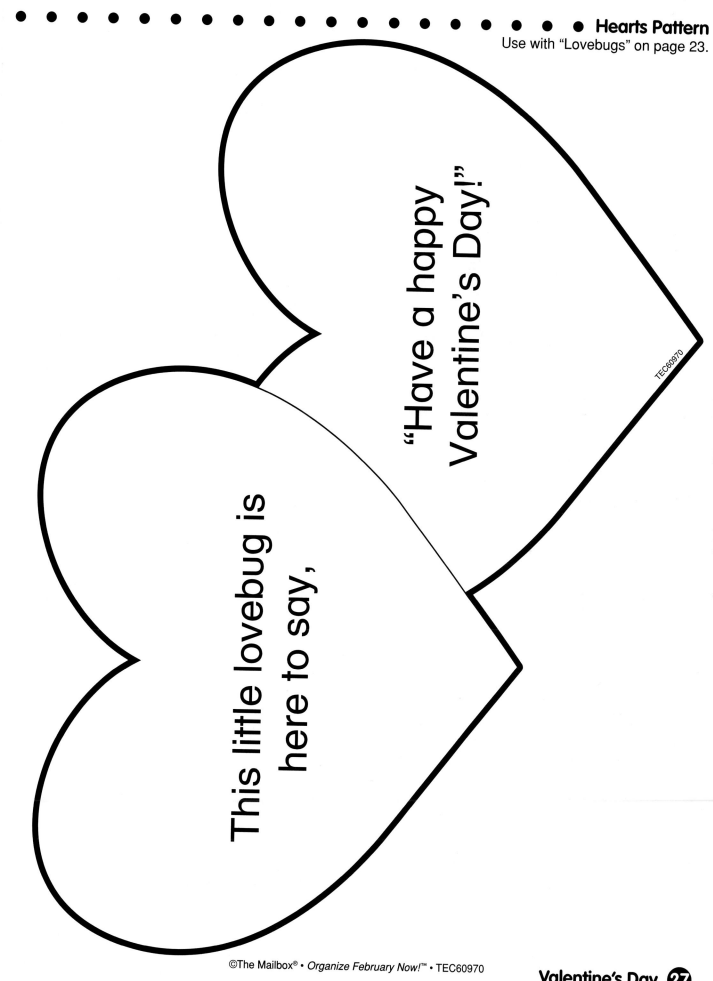

"Have a happy Valentine's Day!"

TEC60970

This little lovebug is here to say,

HEARTS

by _____

©The Mailbox® • *Organize February Now!*™ • TEC60970

Red heart,

1

yellow heart,

2

green heart,

3

blue.

4

All these hearts mean

I love you!

5

Name _____

Color the ☐s red.

Color the ◯s brown.

Heart Partners

Name _____

✎ Color the two hearts in each row that are the same.

Visual Discrimination

Happy Heart

Name _____

✂ Cut. 🔲 Glue the pictures that begin like ♥.

Violet's Valentines

Name _____

Color the pictures that begin like [Be Mine] .

A Beautiful Bouquet: Sponge-paint hearts to resemble a bouquet of flowers on a white construction paper copy of this page. When the hearts are dry, draw stems and additional leaves; then color the bouquet and bunny as desired.

Presidents' Day

Literacy

George and Abe

Introduce youngsters to George Washington and Abraham Lincoln with this presidential booklet. Show youngsters pictures of current and past American presidents. Help each child cut out a copy of the presidents, text box, and booklet pages on pages 39–41. Next, help her glue the patterns and text box near the top of a 9" x 12" sheet of construction paper. Then sequence the booklet pages and staple them below the presidents as shown. Read the text on each booklet page aloud as each child points to the accompanying picture and turns her booklet pages. Invite students to color their booklets and add star stickers or cutouts. Then have each child take her booklet home to share with her family.

Fine-motor skills

Physical Health & Development

Just Like Lincoln

Inform youngsters that long ago, many people lived in log houses. Tell them that as a boy, Abraham Lincoln lived in a log house and went to a log schoolhouse. Then encourage youngsters to make their own log cabin pictures. Have each child arrange 1" x 6" strips of brown construction paper, tearing different lengths as needed, to create a log cabin on a sheet of construction paper. Help her glue the strips and then add crayon and construction paper details, such as a door, windows, or a chimney. Then have each child take home her log house to share with her family.

Celebrate two great American presidents with these star-spangled ideas.

Painting •

Tree Tale

According to the story, George Washington was so honest that he admitted to cutting down one of his father's cherry trees. After sharing this information, invite each youngster to make a cherry tree as a reminder of the importance of honesty. To make a cherry tree, brush washable brown paint on the underside of a child's forearm and washable green paint on his palm. Help him press his arm and hand onto an 11" x 17" sheet of paper to make a tree-shaped print. When the paint is dry, have him make red fingerprint cherries on his tree.

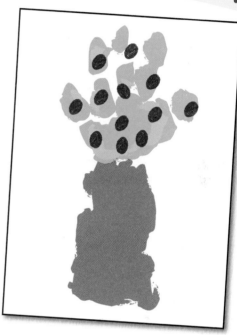

Math • • • • • • • • • • • • • • •

Sorting

Presidential Sort

Count on two famous presidents to boost youngsters' coin-sorting skills. Color and cut out several copies of the coin patterns on page 41. Glue the corresponding patterns back to back. Help your preschoolers identify the coins while guiding them to notice the different presidents. Next, enlist student help to sort the coins according to president. Later, place the coins in a center for independent practice.

A Colorful House

In advance, color a copy of the president patterns on page 39 and prepare them for flannelboard use. Also place on your flannelboard a piece each of red, blue, and green felt to represent rooms in the White House. Show a small group of youngsters a picture of the White House. Guide students to see that the presidential home is white on the outside. Then tell them that inside the White House are special rooms named the Red Room, the Blue Room, and the Green Room. Next, assist a volunteer in following a direction, such as "Place President Washington in the Green Room." Continue in this manner until each child has had a turn to place a president in a special White House room.

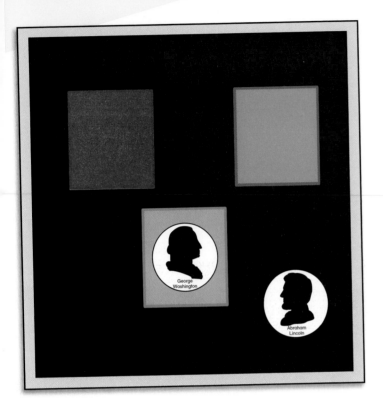

Creative Arts

Drawing · · · · · · · · · · · · · · · · ·

Top Dollar

Introduce youngsters to paper money as they help create this presidential display! Show youngsters several bills as you name each one's president and value. Encourage each child to look at her face in a mirror and then draw her likeness on a four-inch white paper circle. Help her glue the circle onto a 4½" x 8" green paper rectangle and then have her dictate as you record the value as shown. Display the unique bills on a bulletin board titled "We're in the Money!"

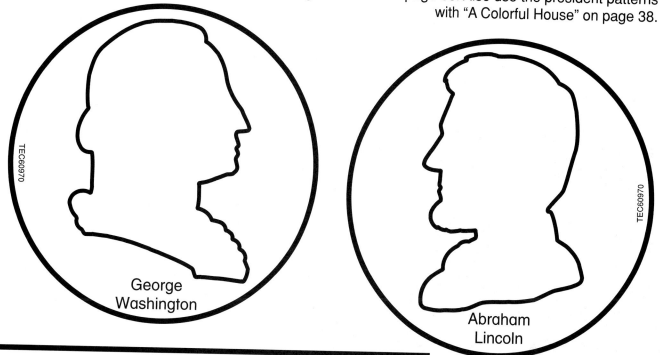

George
Washington

Abraham
Lincoln

TEC60970

TEC60970

Presidents' Day

George Washington lived on a farm.

©The Mailbox® • *Organize February Now!*™ • TEC60970

1

George Washington was the first president.

2

Abraham Lincoln lived in a log cabin.

3

Abraham Lincoln was the 16th president.

4

Coin Patterns
Use with "Presidential Sort" on page 37.

Dental Health

Super Smiles

To prepare for this center, use the patterns on page 46 to make five construction paper smiley faces and 15 construction paper teeth; then cut out the patterns. For each face, draw a different number of teeth (from one to five) along the bottom of each mouth. Place the faces and teeth at a center. When a child visits the center, he chooses a face and counts the number of teeth. Then he matches the number set by placing the same amount of teeth along the top of the mouth. He continues in this manner for the remaining faces.

Nutrition · · · · · · · · · · · · · · ·

Physical Health & Development

Down the Hatch!

Use this tempting sorting activity to help youngsters identify tooth-friendly foods. To prepare, wrap a shoebox and its lid separately with colored paper. On the lid, draw a face with a large, toothy smile. Cut a four-inch slit in the middle of the mouth. Copy, color, and cut out enough tagboard food cards (page 47) so that there is one card for each child.

Present the prepared shoebox to little ones and tell them its name is Big Mouth. Explain that Big Mouth only likes to eat foods that are good for its teeth. Give each child a food card. In turn, help each youngster identify her food and decide whether or not it is healthy. If it is, she feeds Big Mouth by placing the card into the slot. If it is not good for teeth, she sets the card beside Big Mouth.

Little ones are sure to be all smiles when you use
the following learning experiences to recognize
National Children's Dental Health Month!

Oral hygiene • • • • • • • • • • • • • •

Physical Health & Development

Tooth Pals

Good oral hygiene is just a stroke away when youngsters practice brushing with these tooth puppets and oversize toothbrushes! Cut a sealed business-size envelope in half. Give each child an envelope half, a toothbrush cutout (pattern on page 48), and a length of cardboard tube.

Have each youngster draw a happy white tooth on one side of her envelope half and a sad yellow tooth on the other side to make a reversible puppet. Then ask her to color her toothbrush. Help her fringe-cut the head to resemble bristles and glue the handle to the tube, making sure not to glue the bristles. Invite each student to place her puppet on one hand and hold the toothbrush in her other hand. Model good brushing techniques as each youngster practices brushing the sad plaque-covered tooth and then turns it around to reveal a happy clean tooth!

Language Development

• • • • • • • • • • • • *Oral language*

A Tooth Tribute

Sink your teeth into a discussion about dental health by teaching youngsters this action song!

(sung to the tune of "Jingle Bells")

Brush your teeth, brush your teeth, Each and every day.	*Pretend to brush teeth with index finger.*
Brushing makes your teeth shiny And keeps cavities away!	*Point to teeth.*
Dental floss, dental floss, Use it every day.	*Move imaginary floss back and forth.*
Flossing cleans between your teeth And helps keep plaque away!	*Point with two fingers.*
Healthy teeth, healthy teeth, Help them stay that way.	*Point to teeth.*
Brush and floss and eat good foods Each and every day!	*Pretend to brush and floss.*

What's Missing?

In advance, obtain a collection of five or six items related to dental health, such as toothpaste, a toothbrush, mouthwash, dental floss, an apple, and a tooth mirror. Place the items on a large tray and gather youngsters around the tray. Show little ones each item, name it, and explain how it helps keep teeth happy. Allow time for youngsters to study the display. Then have students cover their eyes while you secretly remove one item from the tray. Next, ask youngsters to uncover their eyes and look at the tray to determine which item is missing. Give clues as needed. Once the correct item is named, return it to its original position on the tray and then secretly remove a different item for another round of play.

Language Development

Descriptive language • • • • • • • • • • • •

Sensible Snacks

Serve up a healthy snack to show little ones that foods that are good for teeth come in different shapes, sizes, tastes, and textures. Give each youngster a paper plate with a peeled apple slice, a thin carrot or celery stick, and a slice of cheese. Invite each child to look at his snacks and then touch, smell, and listen to each item as he tastes it. After youngsters eat their snacks, invite volunteers, in turn, to describe the different foods. Record their responses on a chart similar to the one shown. Don't forget to tell little ones that their snacks were not only good for their teeth but good for their bodies too!

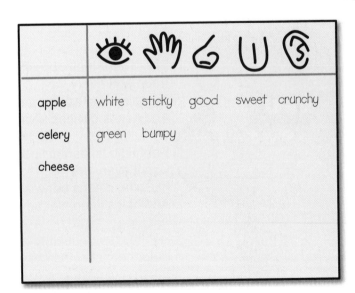

	👁	✋	👃	👄	👂
apple	white	sticky	good	sweet	crunchy
celery	green	bumpy			
cheese					

Physical Health & Development

Flossing Fun!

Not only does this small-group activity help youngsters with fine-motor skills, but it also shows them how flossing helps clean teeth. To begin, squirt a small amount of shaving cream on a foam plate or tray. Invite a volunteer to press one hand on the plate, making sure to get shaving cream between her fingers. Show little ones how to use a length of thick yarn to floss between each finger to remove the shaving cream. Explain that this is similar to what happens to plaque and food particles when teeth are flossed.

Next, give each pair of students access to the plate of shaving cream and a length of thick yarn. Assign one child to be the teeth and the other to be the flosser. Have the flosser clean between her partner's fingers. Then invite youngsters to switch roles and repeat the process.

Science • • • • • • • • • • • • • • • • •

Darrell
brushed _his_ teeth!

Brushing Is Best!

Encourage little ones to brush their teeth with this incentive chart! Give each child a personalized incentive chart and a construction paper toothbrush cutout (patterns on page 48). Invite him to decorate the toothbrush and help him fringe-cut the head to resemble bristles. Next, have each youngster glue his toothbrush and chart to a 6" x 9" sheet of construction paper as shown. Encourage him to take home his chart and color in a box each time he brushes his teeth. Once all of the boxes are colored, have him return his chart to you and then present him with a colorful copy of the badge on page 48.

Find a reproducible activity on page 49.

Smiley Face and Teeth Patterns
Use with "Super Smiles" on page 42.

TEC60970

TEC60970

TEC60970

TEC60970

TEC60970

TEC60970

TEC60970

TEC60970

TEC60970

TEC60970

TEC60970

TEC60970

TEC60970

Toothbrush Pattern • • • • • • • • • • • • • • • **Badge**

Use with "Tooth Pals" on page 43 and "Brushing Is Best!" on page 45.

Use with "Brushing Is Best!" on page 45.

I am a

super brusher!

TEC60970

Incentive Chart

Use with "Brushing Is Best!" on page 45.

_____

brushed _____ teeth!

TEC60970

TEC60970

Terrific Teeth

Name

Color the pictures that begin like 🦷.

Arts & Crafts

Simple Shadows

Your preschoolers will definitely see a shadow on Groundhog Day with this project! Cut out a tagboard copy of the groundhog on page 55. Use rolled pieces of masking tape to secure it to a sheet of black construction paper. To make a shadow, dip a sponge into white tempera paint; then dab paint all around the edges of the tagboard groundhog. When the paint is dry, carefully lift off the tagboard to reveal the shadow.

Puppy Love

These dalmatian pups are sporting some special spots for Valentine's Day! Make a heart stamp by hot-gluing a craft foam heart to the end of an empty film canister. To make a spotted pup, dip the heart stamp into red, pink, or purple tempera paint and print spots all over a white construction paper cutout of the dalmatian pattern on page 54. If desired, make additional heart-shaped spots with other valentine colors of paint.

A Cool Card

Whip up "ice cream" paint by briskly folding two parts nonmentholated shaving cream with one part white glue. Add red food coloring to make the paint pink. Fold until the mixture is stiff and shiny.

To make a greeting card, trim a 2" x 6" piece of tan construction paper to resemble an ice-cream cone. Glue it near the bottom of a sheet of construction paper. Use a craft stick to spread a dollop of the paint on top of the cone, forming it into a heart shape. Shake on glitter to resemble sprinkles. Then allow the paint to dry overnight. The next day, cut out a copy of the text box on page 55 and glue it to the card as shown. Help each child complete his card by writing his name where indicated.

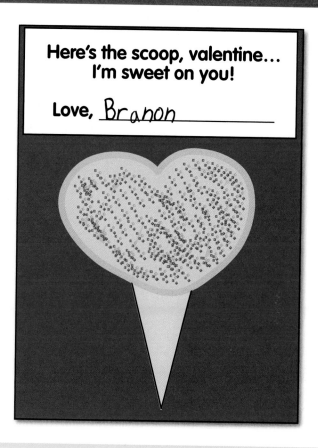

Here's the scoop, valentine...
I'm sweet on you!

Love, Branon

Special Delivery

To make a giant stamp, trim each side of a 4" x 5" sheet of white construction paper with decorative scissors. Sponge-paint a pink, red, or purple heart in the center of the stamp. When the paint is dry, add crayon designs around the heart. Then write a number in the bottom right corner to show the stamp's value. Now that's a special stamp for a special valentine!

3¢

Creatively Crumpled

Little ones discover blending colors with this pretty waxed-paper project. To make one, fold a 9" x 12" piece of waxed paper in half. Then open it and drop a dollop of red tempera paint on one side of the fold and a dollop of white paint on the other side. Fold the paper again and rub to blend the paint colors. Then crumple the paper into a ball. Open it back up and observe the effect of this cool color mixing! When the paint is dry, glue a sheet of 9" x 12" red construction paper with a heart shape cut from its center atop the waxed paper.

By George!

To make a portrait of George Washington, glue a blue hat cutout to a pink paper oval. Use a crayon or marker to add facial features. Next, cut a round white doily in half and glue it to the back of the face, creating a collar. Trim two corners of a 4½" x 9" strip of blue construction paper to resemble shoulders as shown; then glue the cutout in place behind the doily. Finally, glue cotton balls on each side of George's face to make his hair.

Smile!

Celebrate National Children's Dental Health Month with a project that will remind youngsters to take care of their teeth. From old magazines, cut out pictures of smiling faces, toothbrushes, toothpaste, and foods that are good for your teeth. Glue these to a large red smile cutout. Then add a few smiley-face stickers and stamps.

Minty-Fresh Teeth

Youngsters will be brushing teeth with minty paint instead of toothpaste! Mix a few drops of water and a few drops of peppermint extract into white tempera paint so that the mixture's consistency is similar to heavy cream. To make one minty-fresh tooth, dip an old toothbrush into the paint and use it to brush a large tagboard tooth cutout. When the paint is dry, use a permanent marker to draw a happy face on the clean, fresh tooth.

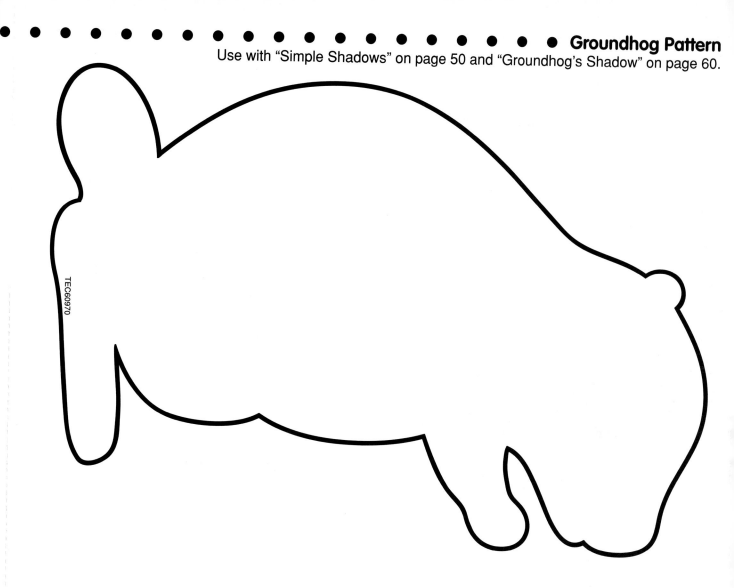

TEC60970

Text Box
Use with "A Cool Card" on page 51.

Here's the scoop, valentine…
I'm sweet on you!

Love, _____

Bulletin Boards &

"Whole-hearted"

To make this extra large display, cut a large heart from red bulletin board paper. Puzzle-cut the heart, making sure there is one piece for each youngster. Have each child create a self-portrait on a paper circle using crayons or markers and yarn. Next, glue each face to a separate puzzle piece and label it with the child's name. Invite little ones to help assemble the puzzle and then display the heart with the title shown.

Invite each child to draw a self-portrait on a copy of the oval pattern on page 58. Assist her in writing her name and the year on a yellow copy of the nameplate on page 58. Then help her glue her portrait and nameplate to a sheet of colorful construction paper. Mount each paper to a slightly larger sheet of construction paper to make a frame. Display the completed projects and the title shown on a board.

Displays

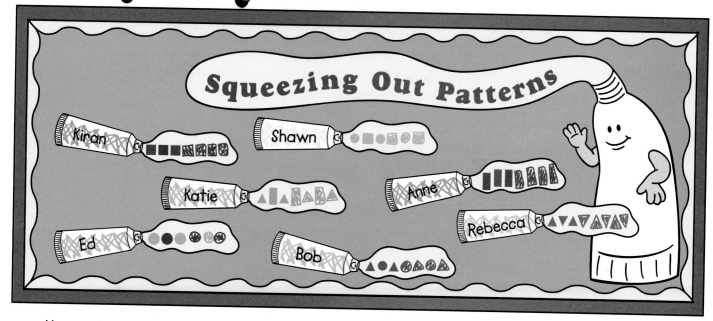

Have each child decorate a personalized construction paper copy of a toothpaste tube pattern from page 59. For each child, cut out a light blue construction paper toothpaste blob and program it with the beginning of an AB pattern. Give each child a pattern and help her extend it. Then mount each toothpaste tube with its toothpaste on a board with the title shown.

Taking attendance is a treat with this display! To prepare, cut a large sack from bulletin board paper and label it as shown. Invite each child to use art supplies to decorate a personalized construction paper heart cutout. Laminate the hearts. Attach the loop sides of Velcro pieces to the backs of the hearts and attach the hook sides of Velcro pieces to the sack. Mount the sack within students' reach and place the hearts nearby. When a child arrives at school, he attaches his personalized heart to the sack.

Oval and Nameplate Patterns

Use with "Preschool Presidents" on page 56.

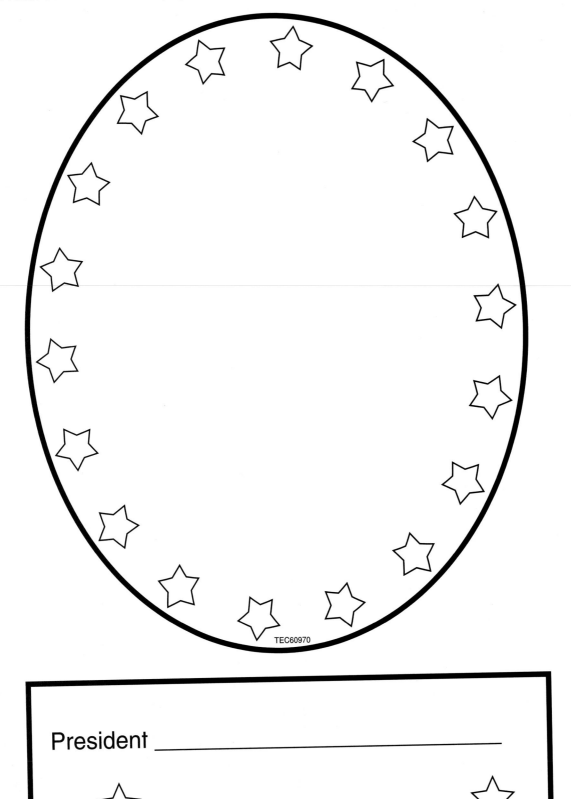

TEC60970

President _____

_____

TEC60970

TEC60970

TEC60970

TEC60970

©The Mailbox® • *Organize February Now!*™ • TEC60970

Literacy

Groundhog's Shadow

The groundhog's famous shadow shares the spotlight with other /sh/ words at this literacy center! To prepare, make a tagboard cutout of the groundhog on page 55. Trace it onto black construction paper; then cut out the resulting groundhog shadow. Place the shadow at a center along with a copy of the picture cards on page 63. A child names each picture card. If the picture's name begins with /sh/ like *shadow,* he places the card on top of the groundhog shadow. If it begins with a different sound, he sets it aside.

Math

Sorting by color

Brush Up

Red, yellow, blue—sorting toothbrushes is easy to do! To prepare this center, duplicate the toothbrush cards on page 64 on three different colors of construction paper. Cut the cards apart and place them at your math center. Invite a child to sort the toothbrushes by color. Challenge older preschoolers to also count the number of toothbrushes in each group.

Fine-motor skills

George's Cherry Tree

After telling your little ones the story of how George Washington chopped down the cherry tree, invite them to create their own cherry trees at your play dough center. To prepare, make a few tree-shaped workmats from brown and green construction paper; then laminate them. Also, scent a batch of red play dough by kneading in some powdered cherry drink mix. Store the dough in an airtight container at a center along with the mats. A child pinches off bits of the scented dough, rolls the dough into cherries, and then places them on a tree mat. For an added challenge, encourage her to count the number of cherries she puts on her tree.

Literacy

Matching lowercase letters

Mended Hearts

These hearts start out broken, but your preschoolers mend them by matching! On each of a supply of construction paper hearts, program each half with a matching lowercase letter. Then cut each heart in half with a different simple puzzle cut. Put all the pieces in a resealable plastic bag at your literacy center. A child mends the hearts by finding the matching letters. Challenge older preschoolers to identify the letters as he makes each match.

Math

On the Candy Trail

Little ones make their way toward a candy castle in this fun game center! Color a copy of the gameboard on page 65. Program each face of a blank cube with a set of one, two, or three dots. Place the cube, the gameboard, and a pom-pom at your game center. To play, a child places the pom-pom on the start space. She rolls the cube and moves the pom-pom the corresponding number of candies along the trail. She keeps rolling and moving until she reaches the castle.

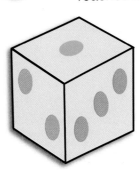

Physical Health & Development

Fine-motor skills

Valentine Bracelets

Making these bracelets is a "hole" lot of fun for little fingers! To prepare, purchase or cut out several different-colored craft foam hearts for each child. Punch a hole in the middle of each heart. Place the hearts in a center along with a class supply of 12-inch lengths of yarn (wrap the ends with tape). A child strings hearts in the colors of her choice onto a length of yarn. When she has a few hearts on the yarn, help her wrap it around her wrist and tie the ends in place. Cut off any excess yarn, and the bracelet is complete!

TEC60970

TEC60970

TEC60970

TEC60970

TEC60970

TEC60970

TEC60970

TEC60970

TEC60970

Toothbrush Cards

Use with "Brush Up" on page 60.

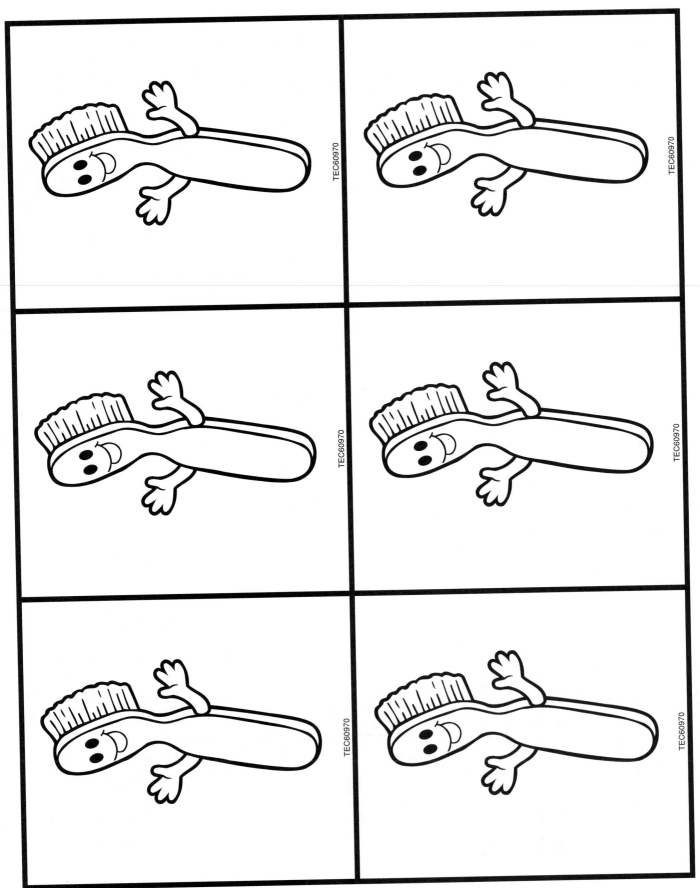

Start

Note to the teacher: Use with "On the Candy Trail" on page 62.

Circle Time & Games

Math

Number awareness

Five Little Groundhogs

Welcome Groundhog Day with this cute poem. Color a copy of the cards on page 68 and prepare them for flannelboard use. Next, teach youngsters the poem shown. As you recite the poem in unison, invite a volunteer to remove a groundhog where indicated in each verse.

Five little groundhogs walking through the door,
One ran away and then there were four.

Four little groundhogs sitting by a tree,
One ran away and then there were three.

Three little groundhogs heard a cow say, "Moo!"
One ran away and then there were two.

Two little groundhogs sitting in the sun,
One ran away and then there was one.

One little groundhog heard a lion roar;
He ran away and then there were no more!

Social & Emotional Development

Self-esteem

You're Sweet!

This valentine version of Hot Potato will have your preschoolers sending out compliments and smiling as they receive them! Seat your students in a circle; then hand one child an empty heart-shaped candy box. Play some recorded music and have students pass the candy box around the circle. Then stop the music. Have the class identify the student left holding the box by saying in unison, "[Child's name], you're sweet!" Then start the music again for more passing and praising!

Understanding feelings

What Is Love?

This creative activity combines movement, thinking skills, and a great gift for caregivers! Teach youngsters the rhyme shown. During the last line, call on one student at a time to tell you what he thinks love is. Write his idea on a personalized copy of page 69. Then repeat the rhyme until you've called on each child for his idea. Afterward, invite each child to illustrate his card and then give it to a special caregiver.

Stand up straight and stomp your feet.
Turn around; now take a seat.
Put a hand on the floor and a hand up above.
[Child's name], won't you tell me, what is love?

Rob says, "Love is my mommy's hugs and bedtime stories."

Math

Three!

Counting

1, 2, 3... Brush!

Here's a game you can count on to raise some interest in toothbrushing! Seat students in a circle and enlist their help in counting aloud as they pass around a toothbrush (or a tagboard copy of the toothbrush pattern on page 48). When you reach a predetermined number, invite the child holding the toothbrush to pretend to brush her teeth. Then begin counting and passing for another round of play.

Groundhog Cards

Use with "Five Little Groundhogs" on page 66.

TEC60970

_____ says, "Love is _____

_____."

Note to the teacher: Use with "What Is Love?" on page 67.

Circle Time & Games

69

Management Tips

Honorary President

The honor of being president for the day encourages good behavior and boosts youngsters' self-esteem! Personalize a colorful construction paper copy of the badge on page 71 for each child in the class. Each day choose one child to wear her badge and act as president of the class. Give the president special duties and privileges, such as leading the line or choosing a story. At the end of the day, recognize the president's accomplishments with a round of applause; then encourage her to wear her badge home.

Sweet Storage

Here's a sweet way to keep the room tidy and recycle at the same time. Collect several heart-shaped candy boxes after Valentine's Day. Store small materials such as math manipulatives or art supplies in each box. Label the boxes and stack them neatly on a shelf.

President for the day!

name

TEC60970

President for the day!

name

TEC60970

Run, Mr. Groundhog!

Welcome Groundhog Day with this frisky fingerplay!

The groundhog sleeps in his winter home,
Below the frozen ground.

While seated, rest head on hands.

In February he pops up
And then looks all around.

*Stand up quickly.
Shade eyes with hand and look around.*

If he sees his dark shadow
In the shining winter sun,

Point to shadow on the floor.

He'll run back into his cozy home.
Run, groundhog! Run!

Run in place; then sit down in relief.

Valentine Friends

Celebrate this sweet holiday with a friendly song!

(sung to the tune of "Do Your Ears Hang Low?")

On this special day
I'll give you a valentine.
It is pink and lacy,
And it says, "Will you be mine?"
I hope we will be friends
For today and all year long,
As we sing this song!

Will you be mine?

Fingerplays

Presidential Poem

Recognize George Washington's and Abraham Lincoln's birthdays with this poem.

February is the month
For us to celebrate
The birthdays of two famous men
Who made our country great.

George Washington was our first president;
He was the best that he could be.
Abraham Lincoln was a kind president
Who made every American free.

Smiling Teeth

Here's a fingerplay to remind little ones to keep their pearly whites healthy!

Your teeth are very important.
You should brush them every day.   *Pretend to put toothpaste on a toothbrush.*
Brush them up and brush them down;   *Pretend to brush teeth up and down.*
Then brush the other way.   *Pretend to brush teeth from side to side.*

Visit the dentist regularly.
Eat fruits and vegetables too.   *Pretend to eat an apple.*
Keep your teeth clean and healthy,
And they'll keep smiling bright for you! *Smile.*

Where's the Candy?

A ready-to-use center mat and cards

Positional words *in* and *out*

Materials:
center mat to the right
center cards on pages 77 and 79
resealable plastic bag or small heart-shaped
   candy box

Preparing the center:
    Cut out the cards and put them in the bag or
the candy box.

Using the center:
1. A child removes the cards from the bag or candy box and lays them pink side up in the center area.
2. He chooses a card, decides whether the picture shows the candy *in* the box or *out* of the box, and then places the card in the matching area on the mat.
3. He repeats Step 2 until each card is sorted.
4. To check his work, he turns over each stack of cards. If each card in the stack has the same symbol on the back, his work is complete. If not, he turns the cards over and rearranges them until they are sorted correctly.

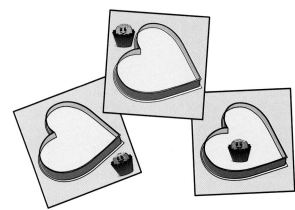

Family Follow-Up
    After a youngster completes the center, have him take home a copy of page 81 to complete with a parent.

Dear Parent,
  We have been learning to recognize pictures that show the positions *in* and *out.* Please help your child point to the heart boxes that have the candy *in* the box. Have him or her color those candies red. Next, have your child point to the boxes that show the candy *out* of the box and color them brown.

Where's the Candy? 81

Sounds Like *Tooth*

A ready-to-use center mat and cards

Materials:
center mat to the right
center cards on pages 85 and 87
resealable plastic bag

Preparing the center:
Cut out the cards and put them in the bag.

Using the center:

1. A child removes the cards from the bag and lays them blue side up in the center area.
2. She chooses a card and names the picture.
3. She decides whether the picture's name begins with the beginning /t/ sound as in the word *tooth*. If it does, she places the card on the box. If it does not, she places it in a separate pile.
4. She repeats Steps 2 and 3 for each card.
5. To check her work, she turns over each stack of cards. If each card in a stack has the same symbol on the back, she proceeds to Step 6. If not, she turns the cards over and rearranges them until they are sorted correctly; then she proceeds to Step 6.
6. She says the name of the picture on each card from the mat, emphasizing the /t/ sound at the beginning of each word.

Family Follow-Up
After a youngster completes the center activity, have her take home a copy of page 89 to complete with a parent.

Dear Parent,
    We have been listening for the sound of the letter *t*. Help your child say the name of each picture below and decide whether it begins with the /t/ sound as in *tooth*. Then ask your child to color the pictures that begin with the /t/ sound.

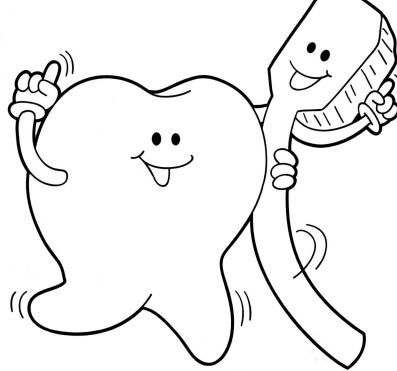

Sounds Like Tooth 89

Lovebugs in the Air

Name

Trace.

Tracing

Special Deliveries

Name _____

🖍 Trace.

🖍 Color.

U.S.
MAIL

Butterfly Beauties

Name _____

Trace.

Color.

Presidential Party

Name _____

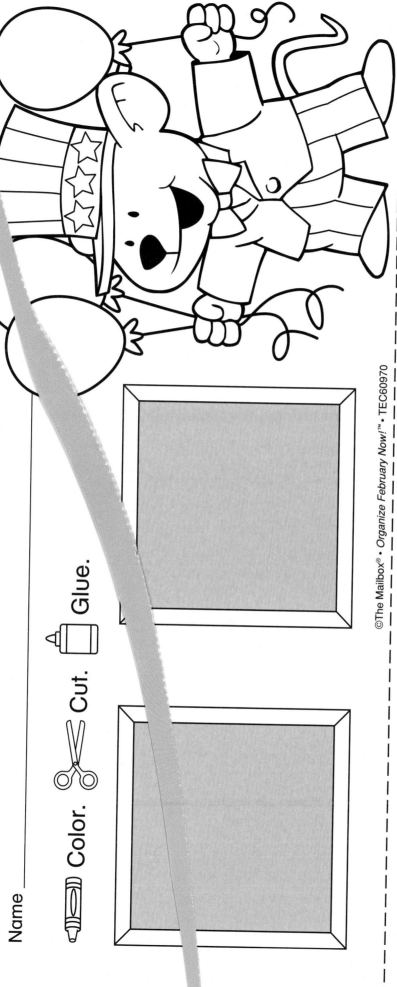

🖍 Color.

✂ Cut.

🍼 Glue.

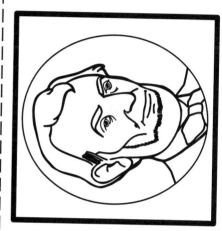

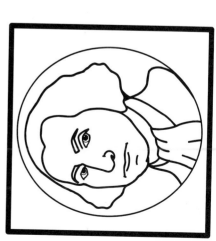

Cupid's Candies

Name _____

🖍 Color.

✂️ Cut.

🧴 Glue.

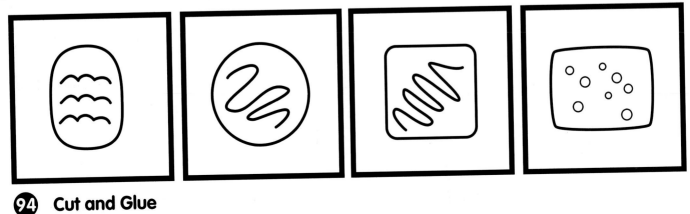

Popping Up!

Name _____

Color.

Cut.

Glue.

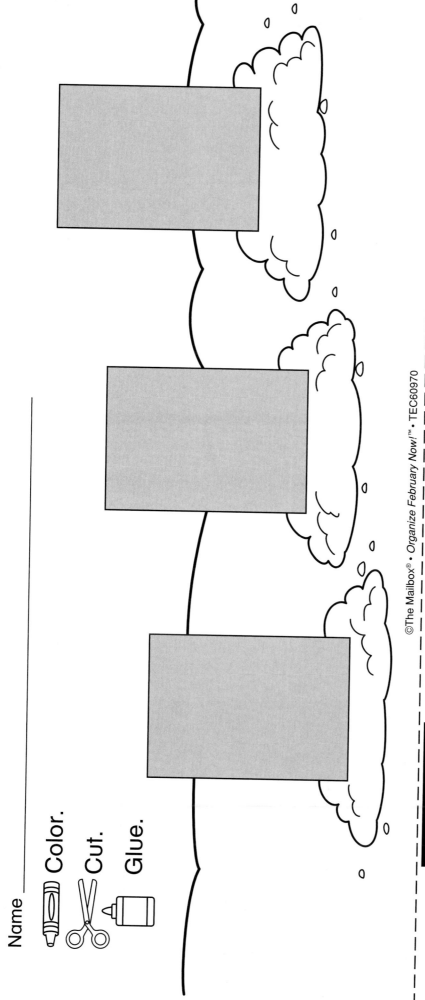

Valentine Vase

Name _____

Color.

Cut.

Glue.

Happy Valentine's Day!